A Guide to Handling Bereavement

Making Practical Arrangements Following Death

Adrian Lewis

Easyway Guides

Easyway Guides
Brighton BN2 4EG

British Library Cataloguing in Publication Data. A catalogue record is available for this book from the British Library.

ISBN 1900694 33 6

Printed and bound by CATS Solutions Swindon England

Cover design by Fred Cowie

A Guide to Handling Bereavement

CONTENTS

Introduction

Death is an unpleasant reality and one that many people avoid thinking about. However, on the death of a person who is close there are very necessary actions that need to be taken.

This book is an attempt to enlighten the reader as to the practical steps that need to be taken after the death of a person. Each step is outlined along with the role of the funeral director and the role of the church and crematoria after death.

The role of the coroner is outlined and also the doctor, registrar, clergymen and cemetery and crematorium officials.

This book does not dwell in depth on bereavement counseling, as this is a separate area and warrants a book on its own. It does, however, outline the process of grief and discuss aspects of this and offers advice in a limited way. The book is very much a practical guide and has been written in the hope that people may benefit from it at this difficult time.

There is a section on non -Christian burial in the recognition that the United Kingdom is a diverse multi-racial society and different traditions apply to different cultures.

There is also a section on wills and probate, as dealing with an estate after death can be very complex and time consuming, particularly if there is no will. Finally, there is a list of useful addresses at the end of the book.

1

Death and the Registration Of Death

If you suspect a person is dead, the first thing that you should do is to tell a doctor. There may be some doubt as to whether the person has died. In all cases, call a doctor or phone the ambulance service. Ask whether the doctor is going to attend. If the death of a person has been expected, then it may not be immediately necessary for a doctor to attend late at night, the next morning will do.

If the doctor does not intend to come, for reasons made very clear, then you need to ask for permission for a funeral director to remove the body. If a decision has been made that the funeral will be a cremation, the doctor will need to know as special papers will need to be drawn up which will involve an inspection, separately, by two doctors. If you intend to keep a body at home prior to such an inspection, which can be carried out in a funeral parlour, then it will be necessary to keep the room at a cool temperature.

Laying out a body

This is the first stage in preparing a body for burial or cremation. In hospital this is called the "last offices" and if carried out by a funeral director it is termed the "first office", denoting either the

11

first or last contact. The body is washed and tidied up, eyelids closed and jaw closed. Hair is tidied, arms and legs And Hair usually grows for sometime after a death so therefore will need shaving. If a funeral director is laying out a body then a gown or everyday clothes will be applied.

Although laying out and general preparation can be carried out at home, and a funeral director can also provide a service in the home it is usual to allow the body to be taken away to a funeral parlor. An occurrence after death is Rigor Mortis, which is a stiffening of the muscles. This begins normally six hours after death and takes effect all over the body within 24 hours, after which it usually begins to wear off. In addition, about half an hour after death parts of the dead persons skin will begin to show dark patches. This activity is called hypostasis and is due to settlement of the blood in the body due to gravity.

Police involvement

In certain circumstances it may be necessary to call the police if a persons death is not due to natural circumstances. It could be that a death is the result of murder or other suspicious circumstance. It is very important not to touch anything in the room as you may disturb vital evidence. The police will take statements from anyone with the person before death. There may at times be difficulty in identifying a dead body and the police have a specific procedure in this case.

Certificate of cause of death

In the United Kingdom, every death must be recorded in the local registrar's office within five days. The Registrar will always require a certificate as to the cause of death. If the cause of death is known then the doctor attending on death will provide the certificate, which states cause, when last seen alive and whether or not any doctor has seen the body since death occurred. This certificate will be given to the family. No charge is usually made.

If the doctor concerned is uncertain about the cause of death or has not seen the body for 14 days after death then a certificate cannot be issued and the coroners office is informed. The body is taken to the coroner's mortuary and a post mortem may or may not be carried out.

The coroner

A coroner is a qualified doctor or solicitor and is paid by the local authority. The coroner is independent of both local and central government and is responsible only to the Crown. The coroner is assisted by the coroner's officer, usually a police officer. The coroner's office has contact with the public.

When a death occurs which is not due to natural causes it must be reported to the coroner. If the deceased died of natural causes but was not seen by a doctor for a significant time before death or after death then the coroner must be reported. The deceased person's doctor will be contacted and cause of death and circumstances ascertained. If satisfied the coroner will cease involvement and issue a certificate and the family can then register the death normally. In any cases where the doctor is uncertain as to the cause of the death then the coroner must be notified. Death resulting from industrial disease, which has given rise to compensation, must be reported to the coroner. In addition, death arising from military service must be reported, in some but not all cases. Other circumstances in which death has arisen which must be reported are:

- If the death was suspicious

- Was sudden or unexplained

- Due to neglect, i.e., poisoning, drugs etc

- Caused directly or indirectly by accident

- Suicide

- In prison or police custody

Another situation is during surgery or before recovering from the effects of anesthetic.

When a death is reported to a coroner, and an investigation is decided upon then a death cannot be registered until enquiries are complete. There will usually be a post mortem. If death is shown to be from natural causes then the family will be notified and the death can be registered normally.

The family of the deceased do not have to be consulted or asked about carrying out a post mortem. If the law requires it then the coroner has to proceed. However, if a family or individual objects they can register that objection with the coroner who has to listen and give reasons for a post mortem. If there are still objections

14

there is the right of appeal to the High Court. This will delay disposal of the body. The coroner has no duty to inform the next of kin about findings of a post mortem.

After the post mortem, and a coroner's report made to the relevant authorities, the body becomes the responsibility of the family.

The coroner is obliged to hold an inquest into every violent and unnatural death and also death whilst in prison. The inquest is open to the public and can take the form of a trial, with witnesses called. The office of the coroner is a powerful office and the intention is to ensure that death was natural and not due to violent or other unnatural means. After the inquest is over then the death can be registered in the normal way.

Information concerning death, including the handing in of a certificate or the informing of the registrar of an extended period without certificate due to post mortem or other examination, can be given at any registrar's office (In England and Wales). This will then be passed on to the appropriate district or sub office.

Registration of death

As stated, in England, Wales and Northern Ireland a death should be registered within five days of occurrence. Registration can be delayed for up to another nine days if the registrar receives written confirmation that a doctor has signed a medical certificate of cause of death. The medical certificate must be presented at the register office in the sub-district where the death occurred. The person registering death must decide how many copies of the death certificate is needed and pay for them at the office. Payment must be by cheque, not cash or credit card. If the death certificate is to be sent to someone else then the details must be given to the registrar. It is possible at this stage for what is known as the "green certificate" authorising burial or cremation to be sent to the funeral director carrying out the funeral arrangements.

Names addresses and phone numbers of local registrars can be found in doctors surgeries, libraries etc.

Registrar's requirements

Registrar's information is contained on a part of a medical certificate issued by the doctor. This part is entitled "notice to informant" and lists:

- The date and place of death
- The full name, including maiden name if appropriate of the deceased
- Date of birth
- Occupation
- Occupation of the husband if deceased was a married woman or widow
- Address
- Whether deceased was in receipt of pension or allowance from public funds
- If the deceased was married, the date of birth of the surviving partner

The form also states that the deceased's medical card should be given to the registrar.

The other side of this particular form gives details of who is qualified to inform the registrar of a death. If the death occurs in a house or any other public building, the following can inform a registrar of a death:

- A relative of the deceased who was present at the death
- A relative who was present during the last illness
- A relative of the deceased who was not present at the death or during the last illness but who lives in the district or sub-district where the death occurred
- A person who is not a relative but who was present at the time of death
- The occupier of the building where the death occurred, if aware of the details of death
- Any inmate of the building where the death occurred, if aware of the details of death
- The person causing the disposal of the body, meaning the person accepting responsibility for arranging the funeral, but not the funeral director, who cannot register the death

The above are in order of preference. If a person has been found dead elsewhere, the following are qualified to register the death:

- Any relative of the dead person able to provide the registrar with the required details
- Any person present at time of death
- The person who found the body
- The person in charge of the body (which will be the police if the body cannot be identified)

- The person accepting responsibility for arranging the funeral

Only a person qualified under the law can inform of the death. If the registrar considers that the cause of death supplied on the medical certificate is inadequate, or the death should have been reported to the coroner, the registrar must inform the coroner and wait for written authority to proceed before continuing with registration.

In cases where a coroner's inquest has been held, the coroner will act as the person informing death.

Registering a stillbirth

A stillborn child is a child born after the 24th week of pregnancy which did not at any time after being completely delivered from its mother breathe or show any signs of life.

In the case of a stillbirth, both birth and death need to be registered. This is a single operation, which must be achieved within 42 days. Those qualified to register a stillbirth are:

- The mother
- The father if the child would have been legitimate had it been born alive
- The occupier of the house or other premises in which the stillbirth occurred
- A person who was present at the stillbirth or who found the stillborn child.

If a doctor was present during stillbirth that person can issue a certificate of stillbirth stating the cause of stillbirth and the duration of pregnancy. A certified midwife can also issue the certificate if a doctor was not present. If no doctor or midwife was present a parent or other qualified person can make a declaration on form 35, available from the registrar of births and deaths, saying that to the best of knowledge the child was stillborn.

If there is any doubt as to whether the child was born alive or dead then details must be given to the coroner who may then order a post mortem or inquest into the death, following which a certificate can be issued.

Loss of foetus within 24 weeks is not considered to be a stillbirth but is categorised as a miscarriage. If the mother was in hospital at the time of the miscarriage, the hospital may offer to dispose of the remains, or to arrange for disposal. But if the parent(s) would like these buried or cremated in the usual way, it should be possible to arrange this with a cemetery or crematorium, provided a medical certificate is completed.

A lot of funeral directors will give their services free of charge on such occasions, although there may be a fee for crematoria that is incurred on behalf of clients.

Some hospitals offer reverent disposal of stillborn and miscarried children, which often involves a simple ceremony led by a chaplain. In such cases there may be no ashes for subsequent burial or scattering.

Death in a hospital

There is a slight difference to the procedures up to the time of registration if a death is in hospital.

The relatives or next of kin are informed of the death by the hospital staff. If death was unexpected, for example, the result of an operation or accident, the coroner will be involved. Usually, all deaths occurring within 24 hours of an operation will be reported to the coroner. The coroner must by law be informed of all deaths under suspicious circumstances, or death due to medical mishap, industrial disease, violence, neglect, abortion or any kind of poisoning. If the person who died was not already an in-patient in a hospital then a member of the family may be asked to identify the body.

In cases where the coroner is involved it will not be possible to issue a medical certificate of the cause of death, but in other cases this is usually issued by the hospital doctor and given to the next of kin. If the person died before the hospital doctor had the chance to diagnose the cause, then the deceased patient's own doctor may be sometimes asked to issue the medical certificate.

The deceased's possessions will have to be removed from the hospital, with a receipt needing to be signed on removal. If the medical certificate of the cause of death can be signed in the hospital then relatives will have to make arrangements to remove the body from the hospital mortuary. This will usually be the responsibility of the funeral director. Most funeral directors operate a 24-hour emergency service. However, there is no need to inform the director of a hospital death until the next morning after death. If cremation is involved, the necessary forms will be filled in at the hospital. The body cannot be removed until this is done. There will be a charge for filling in the forms.

Carrying out a post mortem in a hospital

A hospital will sometimes wish to carry out a post mortem, not involving the coroner. This cannot be carried out without the permission of the next of kin. In cases where a coroner is involved permission is not required. If a coroner orders a post mortem then this is legally required and cannot be prevented. Results are not automatically given to relatives and a request for these may have to be made.

The procedure for registering a death is the same as for a death outside a hospital. The registration however, must be within the district where the hospital is situated.

Where there are no relatives or others to meet the cost of the funeral then the health authority has the power to do so. There are usually arrangements with local funeral directors to provide a simple funeral for the deceased.

The donation of organs for transplantation

Organ transplants help to save the lives of several thousand people per year and some thought needs to be given as to the possibility of donating organs from the dead person. Organs must be removed as soon as possible after death to prevent deterioration, which renders them useless. No organ can be removed for transplantation until a person is declared brain dead, known as "stem" death. In order to determine brain stem death a number of stringent tests are carried out, the criteria of which are laid down by the Royal College of Surgeons. A patient must be under 75 years of age for their major organs to be suitable for transplantation. The patient must be HIV negative and free from major infection. He or she must be of a compatible blood group to the planned recipient of the organs.

Organs that can be transplanted: Essentially, the organs intended for transplant must be in good order. For example, the lungs of a heavy smoker would be unsuitable. The following are the most commonly used for transplantation:

Heart
Heart transplants are considered for those patients with severe cardiac failure who are considered unsuitable for heart surgery.

Kidney
Kidneys are viable for around 48 hours following retrieval from the donor.

Liver
Liver transplants are required for patients with congenital malformation of the liver, hepatic failure, chronic liver disease, some cases of cancer and inborn metabolic errors.

Heart and lung
This particular operation is carried out for people with an advanced primary lung disease, or a condition leading to this, or lung disease arising as a result of cardiac problems.

The pancreas

Pancreas transplants are used for patients with type 1 diabetes. This operation may be solely a pancreas transplant or can be done together with the kidneys.

Lungs

One or both lungs can be transplanted.

Cornea

Damage to the cornea is a major cause of blindness. Cornea grafting is one major solution to blindness. There is no age limit for corneal donation and corneas can be removed up to 24 hours after the heart has stopped beating. Relatives of patients not dying in a hospital who want to carry out their wishes should first of all consult the donors GP or the ophthalmic department of the local hospital.

Heart valves

These can be transplanted following removal from a donor up to 72 hours after death. There are other parts of the body, which can be transplanted including the skin, bone, connective tissue, major blood vessels, fettle cells and bone marrow. When deciding whether or not to donate organs, religious and other cultural considerations will play a significant part. For Christians, organ donation is considered acceptable to Roman Catholics and Protestants. Christian Scientists, on the other hand, object to all forms of transplants. Buddhists do not object neither does the Jewish faith, with the exception of some orthodox Jews. Mormons have no objection neither do Hindu and Sikh. Muslims tend towards prohibition of organ transplants.

The National Health Service Organ Donor Register

This register is a computer data base set up at the UK transplant Support Service Authority (UKTSSA). All transplant co-ordinators have access to the register, and it can be checked each time a donor becomes available. Although relatives of donors are still asked for their permission to donate, the fact that details are on the register and there is a donor card carried, the decision is made easier by inclusion on the register. Any driving licence issued after 1993 may be marked on the back indicating willingness to donate organs. Anyone wishing to be entered onto the register can do so by post or using a form available from doctor's surgeries, chemists, libraries and other public places.
Donation of a body for medical uses

Some people wish their body to used for medical education or research after death. If this was the wish of the deceased then the next of kin or the executor should contact HM Inspector of Anatomy for details of the relevant anatomy school. This should be done immediately after death. Offering a body may not lead to it being accepted due to too many offers or the nature of the death or whether the coroner is involved or how far away the body is.

Donation of the brain for medical research

Brain donation is a separate issue altogether from Organ donation and cannot be included on the NHS register. The Parkinson' Disease Society Brain Research Centre, which is part of the Institute of Neurology at the University College of London must be instructed to the effect that the donor wishes to donate the brain and potential donors must inform the society in advance or leave clear instructions that this should be done in the event of their death.

It will be the responsibility of the medical school to make arrangements and pay for the funeral. The school will make arrangements for a simple funeral unless the relatives indicate otherwise.

Registration in Scotland

In Scotland the medical certificate of the cause of death is very similar to that in England. The obligation to give a certificate rests on the doctor who attended the dead person during their last illness. If there was no certificate in attendance then any doctor can issue a certificate. In most cases the certificate is given to a relative who will then send or give it to the Registrar of Deaths in their area. If a medical certificate of cause of death cannot be given, the registrar can register the death but must report the matter to the Procurator Fiscal.

There are no coroners as such in Scotland and the duties of a coroner are carried out by a Procurator fiscal. This particular person is a law officer and comes under the jurisdiction of the Lord Advocate. The key functions of the procurator fiscal includes responsibility for the investigation of all unexpected deaths including those under suspicious circumstances. If he or she is satisfied with the doctor's medical certificate and any police evidence then no further action will usually be taken. If there is doubt then a medical surgeon will be asked to report.

In most cases, a post mortem is not carried out and the doctor certifies the cause of death after an external examination. In those situations where a post mortem is deemed necessary then permission is sought from the sheriff. Where there is a possibility of criminal proceedings connected to the death then two surgeons will usually carry out the post mortem.

Death whilst in legal custody or at work must be the subject of a public enquiry which will take the place of an inquest in England. If the death is by natural causes, then there may not be a public enquiry.

A public enquiry is held before the sheriff in the local sheriff court. The procurator fiscal examines the witnesses but it is the sheriff who determines the cause of death. When the enquiry is completed the procurator fiscal notifies the result of the findings to the registrar general. If the death has not already been registered then the registrar general lets the local registrar in the district in which the death occurred know of the death.

In Scotland the law requires that every death must be registered within eight days of death. The person qualified to act as an informant is any relative of the dead person, any person present at the death, the deceased executor or other representative, the occupier of the premises where the death took place, or any person having knowledge of the particulars to be registered. The death may be registered in the office for the district in which the death occurred or in the office in the district where the deceased had resided before his or her death. The death of anyone visiting Scotland must be registered where the death took place.

Registering a stillbirth

A stillbirth in Scotland must be registered within 21 days. A doctor or midwife will usually issue a certificate or the person informing can fill in a form 7, issued by the local registrar. In all cases of doubt, the Procurator Fiscal will get involved.

If the body is to be cremated then a certificate of stillbirth must be given by the doctor who was present at the confinement.

Death Certificates

As is the practice in England, the Registrar will issue free of charge a certificate of registration of death which can be used for National Insurance purposes. All other death certificates carry a fee.

A list of fees for the various functions carried out by the registrar can be obtained from any registrar's office, as in England.

Now read the key points from Chapter one.

Key points from Chapter one.

- On discovering a person is dead, always call a doctor

- If the doctor cannot come, you must ask for permission for a Funeral Director to remove the body

- In certain circumstances, it may be necessary to call the police if the death was in suspicious circumstances

- In the United Kingdom, every death must be recorded in the coroners office within five days

- If a doctor will not issue a death certificate then the coroners office must be informed and there will be a post mortem

- In cases where an inquest has been held, the coroner will act as the person informing death

- In the case of a stillbirth the birth and death must be registered within 42 days

- A different procedure applies to hospital deaths

- The decision to donate of organs will be influenced by religious and other matters

2

Steps after Registration

If you need to make arrangements in relation to the dead person's estate then you will need to obtain several copies of the certified death certificate. The cost is minor, currently £3, changing in April of every year. You will find that a separate certificate is needed for application for probate, for dealing with banks and insurance company's etc. Before applying for the death certificate then you should estimate how many you are likely to need.

It is important that you notify the benefits agency about the death as you will need to make arrangements about pensions etc. There may be a number of other benefits that you can claim after death, including help with funeral costs from the social fund. The funeral director may have a stock of the appropriate forms, which you must fill in.

In addition to copies of the death certificate, the registrar will provide another certificate, known as the green certificate to say that the death is now registered and a funeral can go ahead. The funeral director cannot proceed without it. If the coroner is or has been involved in the death then a different process takes place, which will be outlined a little later on.

If a registrars certificate has been issued before registration then the deceased can be buried only, if issued after registration then it can be cremated. The funeral director will forward the certificate either to the cemetery authority or to the vicar of the appropriate churchyard or to the office of the local crematorium.

Copies of a death certificate can be obtained at a later date from the superintendent registrar if more than one month has elapsed or from the registrar if still relatively soon after the date of death.

Applications for certificates by post can be made to the general register office, see addresses at the rear of this book. In Northern Ireland it should be made to the Registrar General. There is a fee, again relatively minor and a stamped addressed envelope will be needed.

3

Taking Decisions about a Funeral

Understandably, those closest to the deceased wish to get the funeral over with as soon as is practically possible. This is a reaction to the death and to bury a person is to disassociate from the trauma of death, or at least from the first manifestations. However, it is important in all cases to ensure that a decent burial is arranged.

In some cases, the bereaved person will have left instructions in a will concerning burial. There is no strict legal obligation to go by the wishes of the deceased however it is usual to do so. If no instructions were left then the burial arrangements will usually be arranged by the next of kin or an executor of a will. If no next of kin can be traced and there is no executor, the hospital will accept responsibility to arrange a minimum priced funeral. Although any capable person can organise a funeral, it is usual in times such as this to enlist the help of a funeral director.

A funeral director by another name is an undertaker. As with all professions, there are associations regulating the activities of funeral directors, The National Association of Funeral Directors, The Funeral Standards Council and the Society of Allied and Independent Funeral Directors.

You should make sure that a funeral director chosen by you belongs to one of the above associations. If you choose an unregistered firm then there may be no comeback in cases of future problems. The function of the funeral director is to assume complete responsibility for organising and supplying all that is needed for a funeral and also to provide as much care as is possible for relatives at this difficult time. Some funeral directors will also offer a bereavement counseling service. It is up to the deceased's family to organise a funeral and contact a director, not the executor of an estate, although in practice the executor will take on this function if requested.

A funeral director will provide a quote for a funeral and you should be clear about this at the outset. As with all services there are varying degrees of service at different prices. Insurance can be taken out for a funeral during an individual's lifetime and there are a number of so called friendly societies who offer plans. Any scheme that you invest in, as with all savings schemes has to be regulated and in the case of funeral plans the regulatory body is the National Association of pre-paid Funeral Plans.

If there is a problem with money, this should be discussed with the funeral director that can assist by encouraging you to apply for a grant from the benefits agency. Normally however, the cost of a funeral is paid for from the deceased's estate.

The price of a funeral will consist of two elements, the fees that the director pays out on the clients behalf-doctors fees, cremation fees if appropriate, fees for the minister, burial fees, gravediggers, flowers and so on. These are the people who provide a service and must be paid. Then there is the fee charged by the funeral director, removal of the deceased, preparation and arrangements, use of the chapel of rest, the hearse and limousine and bearers and so on.

There is a usual minimum price for a funeral starting with a basic funeral for around £700 plus any disbursements, usually around £275 for a cremation and more for a burial due to the increase in activities necessary. As far as price goes, cremation is most certainly cheaper. The average cost is around £200 as opposed for around £400 for a burial. Fees for burials will vary according to the whereabouts of the cemetery. A Church of England Burial tends to be marginally cheaper than others but most graveyards have little burial space left, often involving a second internment in a grave. Some funeral directors will charge for a complete service, including coffin while others will make a separate charge for the choice of coffin required. Funeral director will be able to show clients a range of types of coffin. The material that a coffin is made from varies and will greatly affect the price. Basic coffins are made from chipboard laminated with plastic foil. More expensive coffins are made from solid wood, usually oak.

There are other coffins, made from strong cardboard. However, it is always best to closely inspect the type of coffin you intend to purchase and ask questions about its durability.

Whether you buy a coffin for a cremation or for a burial will also have some bearing on the type that you buy as weaker coffins will normally suffice for cremation. Each coffin must be fitted with a name-plate of the deceased. The plate will also usually contain the age and date of death.

Associated costs

The overall cost of a funeral will consist of the funeral director own fees and those paid to other as disbursements. There may well be extra costs, which are not paid direct to the funeral director, or if paid cover anything extra such as long journeys in limousines, special services etc. Any funeral director should supply you with a breakdown of what a funeral will cost before the funeral. Funeral directors will always explain different charges and conditions in various areas so that you have an idea of costs. It may well be that you decide that you wish to eliminate certain parts of the service to keep cost down.

The fees currently for a Church of England Service are £61 for the service and £11 for a burial in the churchyard. These are liable to change and are for guidelines only. It is always necessary to ascertain the exact cost from the funeral director.

Fees for burial in a municipal city cemetery are likely to be a lot more than this.

Overall, the total cost of a funeral is around £900-1100, which includes cremation. Burial will be more than this. Like a lot of services, different areas of the country will charge different prices and it is best to be sure before agreeing to a particular funeral.

Obtaining help for funeral costs

If a person is on low income and is in difficulties over funeral expenses there is help from the social fund of the benefits agency, although such help is subject to rigid criteria. The applicant or applicants partner must be in receipt of one or more benefit, Income support, Job seekers allowance, Housing benefit, Council Tax Benefit, family Credit or Disability Working allowance. This applies only to the person arranging the funeral. And the person applying for the benefit must be the one arranging the funeral, the next of kin or person described as the next of kin.

The benefit is means tested, and if there are savings of more than £500 these will be taken into account when assessing the grant. If there is a close relative able to pay the costs of the funeral then an award will not usually be made.

If money becomes available out of the deceased's estate then this will be used to pay back the funeral expenses provided by the social fund. The benefits agency form is the SF 200 and the funeral director can also help with this.

The Social Fund Payment will make provision for up to £600 towards the funeral directors fees, which must encompass almost all the costs. In addition a cremation fee will be paid and the costs of certain doctors forms. Although other small payments are made for necessary expenses the money really only provides for a simple dignified funeral. Other extras, which may be desired, are not covered. Details of the extent of help from the social fund can be obtained from the Benefits Agency. The booklet, D49 provides relevant information.

Some local authorities provide a municipal funeral service. The cost is very much less than the average local funeral and details can be obtained from your local authority.

Those relatives of a member of the armed forces who die in service may be able to receive help with funeral costs from the Ministry of Defence.

Where a person dies without relatives, or no one can be traced then the local authority where the person died, or hospital if appropriate, will arrange a simple funeral. Many hospitals maintain a funeral fund and local authorities usually have close links with funeral directors.

The burial

Anyone, whether Christian or not, whose address is within the ecclesiastical parish is, in theory at least, entitled to be buried within the parish churchyard, even if a death occurs away from the parish. Some churches have burial grounds away from the church, where parishioners have the right of burial. Ex-parishioners and non-parishioners with family graves in a parish area have a right to be buried within a particular parish. It is the local vicar or parish priest who will make the decision about burial and also how much to charge.

Those who are resident within the local parish have to pay a fee to the local church for a funeral service in church and burial in a churchyard. There are fees payable for a funeral service in a church and these should be checked with the local church. These fees change on an annual basis and are decided by the church. If the church service is followed by burial in a municipal or private cemetery then the fee remains the same. There is a fee for a burial in a churchyard without having had a service beforehand. No fee is payable for the burial of a stillborn child or for the funeral or burial of an infant who died within one year of birth.

If the ashes are to be buried in a churchyard following cremation there is a fee and if there is to be a further service following cremation then a fee will be payable. This fee does not apply if there is a simple service of committal. There are additional fees, such as grave diggers fees, this being up to £100. This can be more expensive if a funeral director provides the gravedigger.

A vicar will allot the site of a grave in a churchyard. The burial fee does not entitle anyone to the ownership of the grave or any rights of burial there. If you want the exclusive use of a particular plot in a graveyard, you must apply to the diocesan register to reserve a grave space. This is by the grant of a licence called a faculty. The freehold of the ground, in all circumstances belongs to the church. Normally it takes about six weeks for a faculty to be granted. A faculty must be applied for before death. It is too late after death.

Burial in cemeteries

Most cemeteries are non-denominational, and are run and managed by either a local authority or a privately owned company. Particular denominations own a few cemeteries in the U.K and burial places are restricted to members of that denomination.

Some cemeteries will have a section of the ground consecrated by the Church of England, while the opening of new cemeteries is attended by a service of consecration for the whole area.

The fee payable to a member of the Church of England Clergy for holding a ceremony is the same as that for a funeral service in a church. There will be no church fee.

Some cemeteries have ground dedicated to, or reserved for other specific religious groups, and a separate section of general ground. In most cemeteries any type of religious service, or non-service at all, can be held. Many cemeteries have a chapel in which non-denominational services can be held. Some cemeteries will provide the services of a chaplain for burial services on a root basis. There is usually a choice of Church of England, Free Church or Roman Catholic.

Fees for burial in a cemetery vary according to where it is and who owns it. Fees are usually displayed at the cemetery. It is necessary to make enquiries as to what the fees cover and to obtain an itemised estimate of cost. In most local authority cemeteries, a higher fee is required for those who are not resident within the area. These can be double or treble the normal fees.

Cemetery fees are divided into two parts: there is a charge for purchasing the exclusive rights of burial in a particular plot and an additional charge for internment. These charges will vary considerably. Most local authority cemeteries have an application form which the executor or next of kin is required to fill in. All fees must be paid before the funeral and all documents sent. Normally, as stated this will usually be dealt with by a funeral director.

Types of grave

There are different categories of grave in a cemetery. At the one end of the scale are graves without exclusive rights of burial. The person paying for a burial has no rights to say who else may be buried in the grave. The graves are given a number, marked by a number and usually it is not allowed to put up a plaque by the grave. In a few cemeteries, for a small fee a grave space can be reserved for a specific period of time from the date of payment. After this time it reverts to the cemetery.

In most cemeteries it is possible to buy the right to a specific plot for a period usually not exceeding 50 years. Obviously, this is more expensive than the other options. For a private grave, a deed of grant is given for which cemeteries make a small charge. Another type of grave is what is known as the "lawn grave" in which a person has the right to exclusive burial, but can put up a simple headstone leaving the rest of the grave as grass. This grave is easier to maintain and a lot of modern cemeteries allow lawn graves only.

Other burial places

If you want to be buried in ground other than churchyard ground then the law stipulates that such burials be registered. The deeds to land, even freehold, may impose restrictions on use and enquiries should be made to local authority Environmental Health and Planning Departments. There is the right in certain circumstances to a burial at sea which will be discussed a little later. In addition, there is what is known as "woodland burial" where plots are made available in meadowland or other woodland No burial plaque or stone is normally permitted and the emphasis is on a the maintenance of a natural environment.

Cremation

The majority of funerals involve the act of cremation rather than burial. As discussed earlier, cremation cannot take place until the correct certificates have been produced and the death registered. Four statutory forms have to be completed before cremation can take place; one by the next of kin or the executor, the others by three different doctors. Forms are issued by the crematorium. Both funeral directors and doctors normally keep a supply.

The first form, form A is an application for cremation and has to be completed by the next of kin or the executor and countersigned by a householder who knows that person personally. Forms B and C are on the same piece of paper and has to be completed by the doctor who attended the deceased during the last illness.

Form C is the confirmatory medical certificate, and must be completed by a doctor who has been a medical practitioner (registered) for five years or more in the United Kingdom. Doctors must not be related to the deceased or work on the same ward if they are hospital workers. In other words, they should be independent of each other.

Form F is the fourth statutory document has to be signed by the medical referee of the crematorium, stating that he or she is satisfied with the details on forms B and C, or the coroners certificate for cremation. The medical referee can prevent cremation taking place and can order a post mortem to take place or refer the matter to the coroner. Relatives have no right to prevent this post mortem. If they do not want it to take place then they must bury the deceased instead.

When the coroner is involved and has ordered a post mortem, he or she will issue a certificate for cremation. Forms B and C are not required. When a death is reported to the coroner, he or she must be informed at the outset if the funeral is to involve cremation, so that the appropriate certificate can be issued. This is form E and will be supplied as a pink form to the relatives so that they may register and as a yellow form to the funeral director for submission to the crematorium.

If the body of a stillborn child is to be cremated, a special medical certificate has to be issued by a doctor who was present at the birth, or who examined the body after birth. No second medical certificate is required, but the medical referee still has to complete form F. Many crematoria do not charge for the cremation of stillborn children, or infants up to the age of one year.

Fees for cremation

Fees include the charges made by the crematorium, the fees for the doctor's certificates and usually a standard fee for the minister who takes the service. An organist also needs to be paid in addition to other costs. The funeral director will usually pay all fees and charge accordingly. Crematorium fees can vary from £125-£200, with extra fees for those who did not reside in the district of cremation. Doctors who prepare initial forms will usually charge a minimum fee, around £36, which rises each year.

On occasions, when death has occurred in a hospital, the hospital will wish to carry out a post mortem to improve their knowledge of the patient's condition. The consent of relatives must be given and if so, form C will not be required-providing the post mortem was carried out by a pathologist of not less than five years

41

standing and the result known by the doctor who completed form B. Only one fee of £36 will be charged, unless the pathologist was less than five years standing, in which case another doctor must complete form C and the full £72 will be charged. Most crematoria charge reduced fees for children up to school leaving age. You should check the above fees as they change subject to notice. The majority of crematoria are run by local authorities, although private crematoria do exist. Each has its scale of fees and offers a brochure of services and fees, usually having an open day for the public, usually Sunday, as crematoria are open only from Monday to Friday, with occasional Saturdays.

Services in a crematorium

Charges for a crematorium will normally include the chapel, whether or not it is used. Chapels are non-denominational, catering for a variety of religions. Music can be chosen by the relatives. If they wish, relatives can opt for a non-religious funeral. Funeral directors can usually refer you to someone who can organise this.

Cremations and memorials

Most crematoriums will have various forms of memorial. There will be a book of remembrance in which the name of the deceased can be inscribed. Other memorials involve wall plaques, memorial flowers or rose bushes. There will usually be an extra charge for this. Some more sophisticated crematoria have extensive means of remembrance in their landscaped gardens. Again, there will be a charge for this.

Remains

Cremated remains or ashes of the deceased may be scattered in the grounds of the crematorium, taken away to be scattered elsewhere or buried in a local churchyard or cemetery. The crematorium will not usually charge a fee for scattering ashes after a funeral. However, a fee will be charged if ashes are stored and scattered later. There will usually be a fee if the ashes are to be scattered in a crematorium to the one where the funeral took place.

There is a Church of England Charge for the burial of ashes in a churchyard. This is £55, at current prices, increasing annually. A useful leaflet concerning cremation, "Questions People ask" is available from some local crematoria.

Events before a funeral

Most funeral directors maintain a 24-hour service. If death occurs at home or in a nursing home, two funeral directors will arrive fairly rapidly and take the body to the mortuary. It is rare for a body to remain at home between death and the funeral although is possible if requested by relatives. It is recommended that a funeral director be approached as soon as is possible after a death.

When a body is taken by a funeral director then it will lie in a chapel of rest, where the body will lie in a coffin before the funeral. Laying out of a body will almost always take place in the funeral director mortuary. Arrangements need to be made about any jewelry and also clothes, as the funeral director can supply a gown if necessary.

If a person dies in hospital the body is usually taken to the hospital mortuary-although a number of hospitals normally subcontract mortuary facilities to a funeral director.

When a body is removed by a funeral director it will lie until cremation papers have been completed. If a coroner has decided that a post mortem is necessary then the body will be taken to the mortuary in preparation.

When a body is kept in a chapel of rest, relatives and friends can go to see it before the funeral. Sometimes, there will be an extra charge to see the body at evenings and weekends. Some larger firms of funeral directors also have chapels for private prayer, in which a religious service can be held at the beginning of the funeral before the cortege leaves for the cemetery or crematorium.

Embalming a body

The process of embalming is intended to delay the process of decomposition of a body. The blood in a body is replaced with a preservative, normally a solution of formalin. This is similar to a blood transfusion. It is necessary to embalm a body if it is returned to a private house to await a funeral or if the funeral is to be held more than five days after a death and cannot be put into cold storage.

Before a body can be embalmed, a doctor must have completed the medical certificate of the cause of death and the death registered. When cremation is involved, forms B and C must also have been completed.

If the coroner is involved then embalming cannot take place unless permission has been obtained. Embalmers are qualified and no one else other than a qualified person should be used.

The final arrangements before a funeral

The funeral director must have the registrar's disposal certificate before confirming the final arrangements. All of the functions connected with burial or cremation must have been completed and all fees paid.

The funeral director or a member of the family should ask whoever the family wishes to officiate at the service whether they can or are willing to do so, and at the allotted time or date. Services can be held in a church, churchyard, cemetery, crematorium chapel, village hall or any other suitable place. Funeral services can be held anywhere, with no particular form of licensing necessary.

Non-Church of England Funerals

Denominational burial grounds usually insist on their own form of service. For a practising Roman Catholic it is usual for a priest to say a requiem mass in the local parish church and for the priest to take the funeral service.

With Orthodox Jews, the body should be buried as soon as possible once the disposal certificate has been issued. If a man subscribes to a synagogue burial society, he or his wife and children will be buried free by the society in its cemetery.

Orthodox Jews are never cremated, and embalming or bequeathing a body for medical purposes is never allowed. There are usually no flowers. The burial is simple. Reform non-orthodox Jews are not so rigid and permit cremation and flowers.

If a Jew dies away from home it is the responsibility of the relatives to bring the body back at their own expense for the synagogue burial society to take over.
Non-religious services

There is no obligation to have a ceremony at a funeral. It is important to communicate this to the executor or person in charge if this is the case. If a body is to be buried in a churchyard without a religious ceremony, or by someone of another denomination, you should give at least 48 hours notice in writing. Usual fees are still applicable.

If the body is to be buried in a cemetery or cremated without religious ceremony, the funeral director or local authority should be informed. If there is to be no ceremony then usually a few members will attend the funeral and there will be a few minutes silence or with some music played.

Announcements of deaths are usually made in local papers. Sometimes, the national dailies will have an announcement. The address of the deceased should never be inserted in the obituary. A lot of houses have been broken into when a funeral takes place. The press notice should stipulate requirements for the giving of money to the deceased's favorite charity and also for flowers. The time and date and other arrangements for the funeral are included, and these details should be tailored to a families requirements.

When a body is buried, flowers are normally left on a grave after it has been filled in. At a crematorium there will normally be restrictions as to where flowers can be placed.

The funeral

Although it was tradition for the cortege (procession) to travel from the house to the place of the funeral it is just as common, given the prominence of the funeral director, for the funeral to begin from the premises of the funeral director. If the funeral director provides cars for the relatives and friends of the deceased then he or she will organise and marshal the event and arrange departure.

The funeral director should have discussed all the details of the funeral with the family beforehand, and also arrange where people are to be taken after the funeral and also take care of other last minute arrangements.

The funeral director may walk in front of the hearse as it leaves the deceased's house, and as it approaches the church or crematorium. This is both a mark of respect to the deceased and also a practical arrangement as he can direct the traffic. The coffin will be usually carried into the church or crematorium on the shoulders of the funeral directors staff. Sometimes members of the family act as bearers. Occasionally, at the more formal funeral, pall-bearers walk alongside the coffin. This is tradition and is not so often seen.

The burial
If a burial is preceded by a service in church, the coffin is taken

into the church by the bearers and placed in front of the altar. In Roman Catholic churches the coffin is taken into the church before the funeral and remains there until the funeral takes place. After the service the bearers will take the coffin from the church to the churchyard or cemetery. If a burial is not preceded by a church service then the coffin is taken directly from the hearse to the cemetery. The coffin is lowered into the grave while the words of committal are said. A register of burial in the parish area is kept by the church. Copies can be obtained for a small fee.

When someone is buried in a Church of England churchyard, the family is responsible for the grave. Municipal and private cemeteries will employ groundsmen to look after the common parts and also graves. Cemeteries often stipulate the provision of a simple grave in order to keep costs of maintenance down.

A lot of churches have restrictions on the type of headstones and memorials used and it will be necessary to check with the church first before making any decisions.

Cremation

Traditionally, the funeral service prior to cremation was held in church, with the congregation travelling to the crematorium for a brief committal afterwards. It is an increasing practice for funeral services to be held entirely in a crematorium chapel.

When the words of committal are spoken, the coffin passes out of site although some mourners prefer the coffin to remain until the last mourner has left the chapel. During the funeral service, the funeral directors staff will take flowers from the hearse and place them in the floral display area. The funeral director will take appropriate flowers to a hospital or nursing homes after the mourners have left. When the coffin is out of site it is taken to the committal room to await cremation. When the cremation process is complete the ashes are refined separately and placed in containers.

In the process of making arrangements for the cremation, the next of kin or executors of the deceased person's estate can ask to be present when the coffin is placed in the cremator. This is especially relevant for Hindu funerals where traditionally the next of kin would light the funeral pyre. Usually, only two people are allowed.

Each crematorium will keep a register of cremations and again a copy can be obtained for a small fee. When making arrangements for a funeral, clients are asked what they would like to do with the ashes. While most ashes are scattered or buried in the crematorium grounds they can also be removed by next of kin to be scattered or buried elsewhere.

When ashes are removed, the crematorium will normally provide a certificate confirming that the cremation has taken place. If ashes are to be scattered in the grounds of a different crematorium, there will be a fee of up to £30. There is no law regulating the disposal of ashes, they can be scattered anywhere, with consent from owners etc.

Burial in Scotland

In Scotland it is possible to purchase the exclusive rights to burial in a cemetery or churchyard (Kirkyard) plot. A grave is called a lair. Kirkyards are administered by the local district or islands council. Regulations and procedures for cremation are the same as in England and Wales.

Arranging a funeral without a funeral director

It is possible to arrange a funeral without using a funeral director. Most people will want a funeral director to take care of matters after death, due to grief and the wish to arrange matters quickly. However, some people prefer to arrange their own funeral.

If the coroner is not involved, a doctor's certificate as to the cause of death must be obtained and the death registered. The appropriate papers must be obtained and sent to the cemetery or crematorium with a fee. A date and time for the funeral must be arranged. A minister should be approached if they are to conduct the funeral. A coffin must be obtaine1d along with the means of conveying the coffin to the funeral. If a burial is taking place a gravedigger must be hired

With cremation, the papers as outlined in this book must be obtained and a coffin and crematoria arrangements made.

Coffins can be purchased from funeral supermarkets or from a funeral director. It is always highly advisable to purchase a coffin and not attempt to make one yourself. Biodegradable coffins can also be purchased for a fairly low price. These are normally made of cardboard. Details can be obtained from the natural death centre, address at the back of this book.

It is possible to arrange for a burial to take place on your own land-in a garden or a field. Planning permission is not necessary. However, there are other restrictions, one being the level of the water table and if this is likely to be affected. Other difficulties can arise, one being if a family or person decides to move house. A Home Office Licence is required to exhume a body.

As stated, although it is possible to carry out a funeral yourself, without a funeral director, it is not a common occurrence because of the amount of work involved. Many people decide to leave this to a funeral director.

Now read the key points from chapter three.

Key points from Chapter three

In some cases the deceased person will have left instructions concerning his/her funeral. If no instructions were left the funeral will usually be arranged by the next of kin or the executor of the estate. If no next of kin can be traced and there is no executor then the hospital (if appropriate) will accept responsibility to arrange a minimum price funeral.

A funeral director will usually carry out all the arrangements concerning the funeral

A funeral will cost around one thousand pounds whilst cremation is significantly cheaper

The Benefits Agency can provide advice about help towards funeral for those on low incomes

4

Different Funerals

As Great Britain is a multi-racial society, obviously not all funeral and burials are Christian burials. Some space has to be given in a book like this to cover other funerals as they relate to different beliefs.

Muslim funerals

There are specific codes governing Muslim funerals. Muslims live by rigid moral codes and the Muslim funeral will reflect this.

Normally, Muslims will appoint one person to represent them in making arrangements for funerals. Muslims are always buried and never cremated. There is usually no coffin and the body is wrapped in a white sheet and buried within 24 hours of death in an unmarked grave, which must be raised up to 12 inches from the ground and can never be sat or walked upon.

Because of differences between the British tradition and Muslim requirements, one key difference being that a coffin is required in British cemeteries, special areas are sometimes designated by churches and other cemeteries. Because of the need to bury quickly, any requests for post mortem or organ donation are usually refused.

Muslims believe that the soul remains in the body sometime after death, and that the body remains conscious of pain. Bodies are therefore handled with care. Non-Muslims never handle bodies. Embalming is only usually allowed if a body is travelling over a long distance. The family will usually lay out a body and will place a head so that it is facing Mecca. Muslims must be buried facing Mecca. The family will normally perform all rites and blessings, together with the imam, the spiritual leader of the local mosque.

Hindu funerals

There are many Hindu deities, the three main being Brahma, the creator, Vishnu, the Preserver and Shiva, the Destroyer. Hindu belief in reincarnation means that most individuals face death in the hope of achieving a better life next time. Death is therefore relatively insignificant by comparison.

Hindus are always cremated and never buried. Most Hindus bring their dead into a chapel of rest and candles are lit. There are not normally objections to the body being handled by non-Hindu, although there can be many variations on the theme because of the diversity of the religion.

The Asian Funeral Service arranges Hindu funerals and organises repatriation for those who require a funeral by the Ganges.

Sikhs

Sikhism has a lot in common with Hinduism but there is a strong emphasis on militarism.

There are five symbols of faith important to the Sikh. The Kesh is the uncut hair, which, for men, is always turbaned. The Kangha is a ritual comb, which keeps the hair in place and is never removed. The Kara is a steel bracelet worn on the right wrist. The Kirpan is a small symbolic dagger. The Kaccha are ceremonial undergarments, which are never completely removed even when bathing. Sikhs are always cremated and never buried. The family will always insist that their dead are buried with all five K symbols.

After a death, men are dressed in a white cotton shroud and turban, older women in white and young women in red. Cremation will usually take place within 24 hours. The coffin will usually be taken home before cremation for last respects to be paid. The oldest son will press the crematoria button or see the coffin into the cremator. Ashes are scattered in a river or in the sea or taken back for scattering in the Punjab in India.

Buddhist funerals

After death, Buddhists will prepare a person for death and wrap the body in a plain sheet. There are differing customs within Buddhism, as it is a very diverse religion.

Jewish funerals

Orthodox Jews are very strict when it comes to funerals while more progressive Jews have differing attitudes. When a Jewish person dies, the body is traditionally left for eight minutes while a feather is placed in the mouth or nostrils to detect signs of breathing. Eyes and mouth are then closed by the eldest son, or the nearest relative. Many Jews appoint "watchers" this being a person or people who will stay with the body day or night until the funeral, praying and reciting.

The dead are buried as soon as possible. Cremation is not accepted by the Orthodox Jew. Orthodox Rabbis will sometimes permit the burial of cremated remains in a full size coffin, and say Kaddish (prayer) for the deceased.

Jewish funeral are usually arranged by a Jewish funeral agency. Otherwise, the local Jewish community will arrange a contract with a gentile Funeral Director, but under strict Rabbinical control.

The Jewish Counselling Service offers support to those who have lost another. See useful addresses at the back of the book.

Cult funerals

There are an enormous number of different Christian cults in the U.K., including Mormons and Jehovah's Witnesses, Christian Scientists, Scientologists, Moonies and the Children of God. For most there is little or no deviation from orthodox Christian practice.

Some groups became prominent in the 1960's, such as Hare Krishna and will normally adopt Hindu practices.

Now read the key points from chapter four.

Key points from chapter four

Great Britain is a multi-racial society and it is important that those who reside here show sensitivity to the customs of other cultures as they apply to groups in the U.K.

5

After a funeral is over

When a funeral service is finished, there is usually a gathering of family and friends at the house of the deceased. The organising of this event is important as mourners need to be clearly informed about what has been arranged and where it is being held.

The funeral director will submit an account, which is usually very detailed and will require payment within a reasonable amount of time. If the money is from the estate, there should be no problem arranging for the release of the funds to pay for a funeral. Legally, payment of the funeral bill is the first claim on the estate of the deceased, taking priority over income tax and any other claims.

Memorials

Relatives of the deceased often want to place a memorial tablet or headstone in a churchyard or cemetery where the person is buried. There are normally restrictions on the size of the memorial and full details of the restrictions can be obtained from the burial ground.

The funeral director or monumental mason will normally apply to the church or cemetery authorities for permission to erect a memorial. After a burial, several months should be allowed for settlement before any memorial is erected or replaced. Time and consideration should be given to a memorial, and names of Burial Authorities. The cost of memorial will vary enormously, depending on what has been purchased and a written estimate should be obtained before any order is given.

After cremation

About one week after cremation has taken place, the crematorium will usually send a brochure to the next of kin explaining what kinds of memorials are available. These are all optional and are not covered by the fees paid for the cremation.

The most popular means of memorial at the cremation is the book of remembrance. Hand lettered inscriptions in the book usually consist of the name, date of death, and a short epitaph. The charge depends on the length of entry.

The crematorium displays the book, open at the right page, on the anniversary of the funeral. The crematoria will provide a list of charges on request.

Some crematoria have a colonnade of niches for ashes called a columbarium. The ashes are either walled in by a plaque or left in an urn by the niche. Charges for this are high, where space can be found.

In addition to the above, some crematoria have memorial trees, or rose bushes. These are usually arranged in beds, where the memorial bush is chosen by the family, the ashes are scattered around it, and a small plaque placed nearby. Costs vary and can be provided by the crematoria in question.

Charitable donations

An increasing number of people will request that family and friends make a charitable donation to a nominated charity in memory of the deceased and will regard this as a fitting memorial for the person concerned. Usually, the funeral director will arrange to collect and forward donations and will not charge for this service.

6

The Estate of the Deceased-Applying for Probate

Applying for probate

Probate simply means that the executor's powers to administer the estate of a dead person have been officially confirmed. A document called a "Grant of Representation" is given which enables those administering the estate to gain access to all relevant information, financial or otherwise concerning the person's estate.

Although anyone charged under a will to act on behalf of the dead persons estate has automatic authority to represent, there are certain cases where evidence of probate is required. If no will exists or no executors have been appointed, then it will be necessary to obtain "letters of administration" which involves a similar procedure.

Under common law, probate has a number of objectives. These are:

- To safeguard creditors of the deceased

- To ensure reasonable provision is made for the deceased's dependants

- To distribute the balance of the estate in accordance with the intentions of the person whose will it is.

One of the key factors affecting the need to obtain probate is how much money is involved under the terms of a will. Where the sums involved are relatively small then financial institutions and other organisations will not normally want to see evidence of probate. However, it should be remembered that no on is obliged to release anything relating to a dead person's estate unless letters of administration or documents of probate can be shown. Those responsible for administering the estate must find out from the organisations concerned what the necessary procedure is.

Applying for probate

Where a will is in existence and executors have been appointed then any one of the named people can make the application. Where a will is in existence but no executors have been appointed, then the person who benefits from the whole estate should make the application. This would be the case where any known executor cannot or will not apply for probate.

Where there is no will in existence then the next of kin can apply for probate. There is an order of priority relating to the application:

- The surviving spouse

- A child of the deceased

- A parent of the deceased

- A brother or sister of the deceased

- Another relative of the deceased

The person applying for probate must be over eighteen. Children includes any that are illegitimate. If a child dies before the deceased then one of his or her children can apply for probate.

Application for probate

This can be done through any probate registry or office. There is usually one in every main town and any office in any area will accept the application. If you are writing then you should always address your correspondence to a registry and not an office. You can also contact the Probate Personal Application Department at Somerset House in London, address as follows:

Probate Personal Application Department
2nd Floor
Somerset House
Strand
London
WC2R ILP
Tel: 0207 936 6983

What needs to be done next

The next of kin should register the death with the register of Births and Deaths. A death certificate will be supplied and copies of the death certificate, which will need to be included to various institutions and organisations.

A copy of the will has to be obtained. The whereabouts should be known to the executors. The executor should then take a copy of the will in case the original is lost. The executor will need to obtain full details of the dead person's estate, including all property and other items together with a current valuation. It is possible that on many of the less substantial items a personal valuation can be made. It should however, be as accurate as possible.

In the case of any bank accounts a letter should be sent by the executor to the bank manager, stating that he is the executor and giving full details of the death. Details should be requested concerning the amount of money in the dead person's account(s) together with any other details of valuables lodged with the bank.

The bank manager may be able to pass on information concerning holdings in stocks and shares. If share certificates are held then a valuation of the shares at time of death should be requested.

In the case of insurance policies, the same procedure should be followed. A letter should be sent to the insurance company requesting details of policies and amounts owed or payable.

In the case of National Savings Certificates the executor should write to the Savings Certificate Office in Durham and ask for a list of all certificates held, date of issue and current value. In the case of Premium Bonds a letter should be sent to the Bond and Stock Office in Lancashire Giving name and date of death. Premium Bonds remain in the draw for 12 months after death, so they can be left invested for that time or cashed in when probate has been obtained. Form SB4 (obtained from any post office) is used to inform of death and obtain repayment of most government bonds.

In the case of property, whatever valuation is put on a property the Inland Revenue can always insist on its own valuation. If there is a mortgage, the executor should write to the mortgagee asking for the amount outstanding at the time of death.

The above procedure should be followed when writing to any one or an organisation, such as a pension fund, requesting details of monies owed to the dead person.

Debts owed by the person

The executor will need to compile a list of debts owed by the dead person as these will need to be paid out of the estate. These debts will include all money owed, loans, overdrafts, bills and other liabilities. If there is any doubt about the extent of the debts then the executor can advertise in the London Gazette and any newspaper, which circulates in the area where the estate is situated. Efforts also have to be made to locate creditors outside of advertising. The advert will tell creditors that they have to claim by a certain date after which the estate will be administered having obtained probate.

Funeral expenses should be quantified and a letter should be sent to the Inland Revenue to determine the income tax position of the dead person.

Application for Probate

The executor obtains the application form, decide where he or she wishes to be interviewed, send the completed form together with the death certificate and the original will to the Probate Registry and then attend for an interview.

The forms

The forms consist of the following:

Form PR83-Probate Application form

CAP 44-Return of the whole estate

CAP 37 and 40-Inland Revenue Capital Taxes Office

There will be instructions on application as to how to fill these forms in. It may be possible for an interview to take place on the same day as the forms are received by the appropriate office. The forms can be delivered either personally or by post.

The interview

The interview is to iron out any problems with the application and to get the executor to swear or affirm before the Probate Officer that the information in the forms is true (to the best of knowledge). The taxation form for inheritance purposes has to be signed so that it can be returned to the Inland Revenue for assessment. Probate fees have to be paid at the interview. These are worked out on the value of the net estate. A list of current fees can be obtained from any Probate Office. After the interview the Probate Registry will send the account of the estate to the capital taxes office for an assessment of any inheritance tax payable.

Once the Probate Registry has received an assessment then this will be sent to the executor who should then make arrangements for payment.

The tax should be paid before Probate is granted or letters of administration are given. It must be paid within six months of the date of death.

After a few weeks, the executor will receive grant of Probate. This is simply a sheet of paper which details that the dead person, of a particular address died on a particular day and that the executor has been granted the administration of the estate. The gross and net alue at a specific date are stated. Attached is the probate copy of the will. The executor receives the original death certificate. All probate documents become public property which are open for inspection by the public. Further copies of probate documents can be obtained for a fee.

Now read the key points from Chapter six

Key points from Chapter six

- Probate means that the executor's powers to administer the estate of the dead person have been officially confirmed

- Probate has a number of objectives under the law-to safeguard the creditors of the deceased, to ensure reasonable provision is made for the deceased's dependants and to distribute the balance of the estate in accordance with the intentions of the person whose will it is

- One of the key factors affecting the need to obtain probate is how much money is left under the will

7

The Intervention of the Courts

Courts have wide powers to make alterations to a persons will, after that persons death. It can exercise these powers if the will fails to achieve the intentions of the person who wrote it, as a result of a clerical error or a failure to understand the instructions of the person producing the will. In addition, if mental illness can be demonstrated at the time of producing the will then this can also lead to the courts intervening.

In order to get the courts to exercise their powers, an application must be made within six months of the date on which probate is taken out. If gifts or other are distributed and a court order is made to rectify the will then all must be returned to be distributed in accordance with the court order.

If any part of a persons will appears to have no meaning or is ambiguous then the court will look at any surrounding evidence and the testators intention and will rectify the will in the light of this evidence.

The right to dispose of property

In general, the law allows an unfettered right to dispose of a persons property as they choose. This however is subject to tax and the courts powers to intervene. The law has been consolidated in the Inheritance (Provision for Family and Dependants Act) 1975. Certain categories of people can now apply to the court and be given money out of a deceased persons will. This can be done whether there is a will or not.

The husband or wife of a deceased person can be given any amount of money as the court thinks reasonable. The 1975 Act implemented the recommendations of the Law Commission that felt that a surviving spouse should be given money out of an estate on the same principles as a spouse is given money when there is a divorce. This means that, even if a will is not made, or there are inadequate provisions then a surviving spouse can make an application to rectify the situation.

The situation is different for other relations. They can apply to the court to have a will rectified but will receive far less than the spouse. The following can claim against a will:

- The wife or husband of the deceased
- A former wife or former husband of the deceased who has not remarried
- A child of the deceased

Any person who is not included as a child of the deceased but who was treated by the deceased as a child of the family in relation to any marriage during his lifetime

Any other person who was being maintained, even if only partly maintained, by the deceased just before his or her death

Former spouse

There is one main condition under which a former spouse can claim and that is that they have not remarried. In addition, such a claim would be for only essential maintenance that would stop on remarriage. There is one key exception, that is that if your death occurs within a year of divorce or legal separation, your former spouse can make a claim.

Child of the deceased

As the above, any claim by children can only be on the basis of hardship.

Stepchildren

This includes anyone treated as your own child and supported by you, including illegitimate children or those conceived before, but not born till after, your death. The claim can only cover essential maintenance.

Dependants

This covers a wide range of potential claimants. Maintenance only is payable. There needs to be evidence of full or partial maintenance prior to death. Such support does not have to be financial, however.

There is another situation where the court can change a will after your death. This relates directly to conditions that you may have imposed on a beneficiary in order to receive a gift that are unreasonable. If the court decides that this is the case, that particular condition becomes void and does not have to be fulfilled.

If the condition involved something being done before the beneficiary receives the gift then the beneficiary does not receive the gift. If the condition involved something being done after the beneficiary received the gift then the beneficiary can have the gift without condition.

If the beneficiary does not receive the gift, as in the above, then either the will can make alternative provision or the gift can form part of the residue of the estate.

Unreasonable conditions can be many, one such being any condition that provides reason or incentive to break up a marriage, intention to remain celibate or not to remarry or one that separates children.

There are others that impinge on religion, general behaviour and crime. An unreasonable condition very much depends on the perception of the beneficiary and the perception of the courts.

A beneficiary can lose the right to a bequest, apart from any failure to meet conditions attached to a bequest. Again, a court will decide in what circumstance this is appropriate. Crime could be a reason, such as murder, or evidence of coercion or harassment of another person in pursuit of selfish gain.

8

Welfare Benefits after Death

After the death of a spouse, you may be entitled to a number of benefits from the state. The benefits agency administers all social security benefits and explanatory leaflets are available.

Some of the benefits available are paid only to those dependants of people who had paid, or had credited to them, National Insurance Contributions during their lifetime. The number of contributions required varies according to the type of benefit. Reduced rates are paid in certain circumstances.

Benefits can be paid after someone has died abroad. Write to the Overseas Branch of the Department of Social Security.

Assistance with funeral expenses

If you or your partner together, are getting Income Support, Income Based Jobseeker's allowance, Family Credit, Disability Working Allowance, Council Tax Benefit or Housing Benefit, you may be able to get assistance with the funeral costs if it is seen as reasonable that you should bear responsibility for the funeral and associated costs.

The Social Fund will, subject to certain criteria, meet specified costs, including burial and cremation costs plus up to £600 for other funeral costs. It has to be borne in mind that the social fund will not pay for anything other than the essential costs, these do not include items such as newspaper insertions or any other costs such as flowers and so on.

If you or your partner have savings of over £500 this is taken into account. (£1000 for those 60 or over). You should however, check these figures as they are subject to frequent change. Other sources of funding such as life insurance policies, are also taken into account. The Social Fund Allowance is not treated as a loan as such, but is repayable from the deceased person's estate if there is money to do so. Claims should be made on form SF200 available from the benefits agency or the funeral directors and must be sent in with a copy of the funeral directors account. Your local Social office will supply you with the address of the relevant office to forward the form to.

It is most important to check with the Department of Social Security concerning the range and types of benefits available and also the amounts. The information in this book is for guidance only.

Widows Benefit

Widow's benefit is available to a woman who was married to the deceased at time of death. It is dependent on National Insurance Contributions and is for a woman only. No such benefit exists for the male widower. If a divorce is in process, widow's benefit will not be affected unless a decree absolute has been granted.

A form BW1 must be filled in or by applying for it on the form used to register death. It is very important that the form is sent off as soon as possible, not later than three months after death.

Widows benefit is not affected by any earnings that a widow may have or any income from investments It is subject to Income Tax and may be affected by other benefits payable, such as War Widows pension.

For benefit amounts and National Insurance Contribution details you should contact your local Social Security Office.

Widows Payment

A woman under the age of 45 may get a lump sum payment of £2000 if her husbands National Insurance Contributions were up to date.

Widows Pension

A widow who is over 45 but under pensionable age and who has no dependant children may receive a weekly pension in addition to widow's payment, dependant on her husbands NI contributions.

Widowed Mothers Allowance

A widow who is under 60 with one or more dependant children, or who is pregnant with her late husbands baby, will not receive widows pension, but will instead be eligible to receive Widowed Mothers Allowance. As well as receiving a weekly sum for herself, she will also receive an additional allowance for each child under school leaving age, or who is under 19 and a full time student or who is apprenticed, or whose schooling or apprenticeship has been interrupted because of illness. A widow can claim the extra allowance only for a child who was or would have been treated as part of her late husbands family and normally only for a child living with her.

A widow continues to receive the widowed mothers personal allowance if any child over 16 but under 19 who has left school is still living with her. She does not receive an additional allowance for the child. A widow who is under 45 at the time when her children cease to qualify her for Widowed Mothers Allowance then receives nothing. A widow who is over 45 at that time and under 60 may receive the appropriate Widows Pension for her age at that time.

Widows over 60

A widow who is over 60 and under 65 whose husband was not getting Retirement Pension may be eligible for Widows Payment together with either Widows Pension or Retirement Pension. If her husband had been receiving Retirement Pension she will not be eligible to receive Widows Payment, but may be eligible for either Widows Pension or Retirement Pension. In both cases, the Retirement Pension will normally be paid.

A widow who is over 65 whose husband had not been receiving Retirement Pension may be eligible for Widows Payment and Retirement Pension. If her husband had been receiving Retirement Pension she will not receive widow's payment, but may be eligible for Retirement Pension.

If a woman is 60 or over at the time of her husbands death and they has both been drawing Retirement Pension, she can apply for her Retirement Pension to be changed to the rate for a widow. She may also be entitled to extra basic pension if her husband had deferred his retirement until he was after 65. She will also receive half of any graduated pension that she was getting.

If a widow is already drawing a Retirement Pension based on her contributions, but a pension based on her late husbands contributions would be at a higher rate than her own, she may apply for her pension to be replaced by the higher rate.

Widow under 60 without dependant children

The pension received by a widow depends on age at the time of her husband's death. (different rules apply to deaths before April 1988). If a woman is under 45 when her husband dies, she does not receive a widow's pension. A woman who was 45 or over but under 55 when her husband died is eligible to receive a widow's pension calculated on a sliding scale according to her age. This scale starts at 30% of the standard rate for a woman aged 45 at that time and increases in seven per cent steps, so that a widow aged 54 when her husband died is eligible to receive 93% of the standard rate. A woman who is 55 or over but under 60 at the time of her husbands death may receive the full standard rate of the basic pension.

State Earnings Related Pension

In addition to the standard Widows Pension, a woman may also receive and additional pension based on her husband's earnings as an employed person from April 1978. This pension will be worked out according to a sliding scale revised annually. If her husband was a member of a contracted out occupational pension scheme, part of the widow's additional pension will be paid by that scheme. A widow can inherit the whole of her late husbands basic and SERPS pension. If she is entitled to a retirement pension based on her own contributions, she can add the two Retirement Pensions together.

A man whose wife dies when they are both over retirement age can draw a pension derived partly from her contribution record and partly from his own, in exactly the same way that a widow can do, up to the same maximum.

A woman who is not yet drawing Retirement Pension when her husband dies may qualify for a widows pension, even if she goes on working. Once she has retired, or reached the age of 65, she may inherit half her husbands graduated pension to add to her Retirement Pension as well as any graduated pension of her own.

War Widows Pension

A woman whose husband served in the armed forces and whose death was a result of military service, or who had been drawing war pension constant attendance allowance, should write to the war pensions agency (address at rear of book) explaining the circumstances fully, and asking if she is entitled to a war widows pension.

Other state benefits

A widow whose income and savings are below certain defined levels may be able to claim benefits to top up her income. Advice can be obtained from the Benefits Agency or from Citizens Advice Bureau.

Other benefits, which can be obtained, are:

Income support-a widow who works less than 16 hours per week and has less than £8000 savings can claim income support if her weekly income is below a certain amount

Family Credit-a widow who works for 16 hours per week or more, has dependent children and has savings of less than £8000 can apply for Family Credit if her weekly income is below a certain amount

Housing Benefit-a widow whose savings are below £16000 may be able to claim Housing Benefit to help her pay her rent and council tax if her income is below a certain amount, which varies according to circumstances

Industrial Injuries Disablement Benefit-if a widows husband did not meet or fully meet NI contributions conditions, they may be treated as satisfied if the death was as a result of industrial injury, accident or disease

Jobseeker's allowance-a widow who is unemployed and able to look for work may be eligible to receive jobseeker's allowance

Orphans-a person who takes an orphaned child into a family may be entitled to a guardian's allowance. It is not necessary to be a legal guardian to apply. There are various criteria dealing with this which should be verified with the DSS

Home Responsibilities Protection-a widow who is looking after a child or a sick or disabled person, and either does not work at all or works but does not pay enough NI Contributions in a tax year to make that count for Retirement Pension Purposes may benefit from home responsibilities protection. This is a special arrangement to protect basic Retirement pensions.

Information concerning all of the above may be obtained from the Benefits Agency.

Useful Addresses

There are a number of agencies that provide help to those who have experienced bereavement. Below is a list of the key agencies with addresses and phone numbers.

Age Concern
England
Astral House 1268 London Road
Norbury
London SW16 4ER
Tel: 0208 679 8000
Fax: 0208 679 6069

Scotland
113 Rose Street
Edinburgh EH2 3DT
Tel: 0131 220 3345
Fax: 0131 220 2779

Northern Ireland
3 Lower Crescent
Belfast BT7 1NR

Wales
4th Floor, Cathedral Road
Cardiff CF1 9SD
Tel: 01222 371566
Fax: 01222 399562

Age Concern Funeral Plan
Tel 0800 387735 (freephone)
0208 765 7233 (general enquiry's)

Asian Funeral Service
209 Kenton road
Harrow
Middlesex HA3 OHD
Tel: 0208 909 3737
Fax: 0208 909 3435

Association of Burial Authorities
139 Kensington High Street
London W8 6SU
Tel: 0207 937 0052
Fax: 0207 937 1393

British Organ Donors Society
(Body)
Balsham,
Cambridge CB1 6DL
Tel/Fax 01223 893636

Cremation Society
2nd Floor, Brecon House
16-16a Albion Place
Maidstone ME 14 5DZ
Tel: 01622 688292/3
Fax: 01622 686698

Cruse-Bereavement Care
Cruse House, 126 Sheen Road
Richmond, TW9 1UR
Tel: 0208 940 4818
Fax: 0208 940 7638

Foundation for the Study of Infant Death
14 Halkin Street
London SW1X 7DP
Tel: 0207 235 0965
Fax: 0207 823 1986

Funeral Ombudsman Scheme
26-28 Bedford Row
London WC1R 4HE
Tel: 0207 430 1112
Fax: 0207 430 1012

Funeral Planning Council
Melville House
70 Drymen Street
Beardsmen, Glasgow
G61 2RP

Funeral Standards Council
30 North Road
Cardiff CF1 3DY
Tel: 01222 382046

General Register Office
PO Box 2, Southport
Merseyside PR8 2JD
Tel: 0151 471 4200
Fax: 0151 471 4523

Inquest
Ground Floor
Alexandra National house
330 Seven Sisters Road
London N4 2PJ
Tel: 0208 802 7430 Fax: 802 7450

Institute of Family Therapy
24-32 Stephenson Way
London NW1 2HX
Tel: 0207 391 9150
Fax: 0207 391 9169

IRIS Fund for the Prevention of Blindness
2nd Floor, York House
199 Westminster Bridge Road
London SE1 7UT
Tel: 0207 928 7743
Fax: 0207 928 7919

Jewish Bereavement Society
PO Box 6748
London N3 3BX
Tel/Fax: 0208 349 0839

Lesbian and Gay Bereavement Project
Vaughan Williams Centre
Colindale Hospital
London NW9 5HG
Tel: 0208 200 0511
Helpline: 0208 455 8894

National Association of Funeral Directors
618 Warwick Road
Solihull
West Midlands B91 1AA
Tel: 0121 711 1343
Fax: 0121 711 1351

National Association of Memorial Masons
27a Albert Street
Rugby, CV21 2SG
Tel: 01296 434750
Fax: 01788 542276

National Association of Pre-Paid Funeral Plans
618 Warwick Road
Solihull
West Midlands B91 1AA
Tel: 0121 711 1343 Fax: 0121 711 1351

National Association of Widows
54-57 Allison Street
Digbeth Birmingham B5 5TH
Tel: 0121 643 8348

NHS Organ Donor Register
U.K. Transplant Support Service
Authority, Foxden Road, Stoke
Gifford, Bristol, BS34 8RR
Tel: 0117 975 7575

Overseas Branch of the Department of Social Security
POBD, Benton Park Road
Longbenton, Newcastle upon Tyne,
NE12 9SG
Tel: 0191 213 5000

Public Search Room
Family Records Centre
1 Myddleton Street
London EC1R 1UW
Tel: 0208 392 5300
Certificate enquiry's 0171 233 9233

Registrar General (Northern Ireland)
GRO Oxford House
49-55 Chichester Street, Belfast
BT1 4HH
Tel: 01232 252000
Fax: 01232 252044

Society of Allied and Independent Funeral Directors
Crowndale House
1 Ferdinand Place London NW1 8EE
Tel: 0207 267 6777

INDEX